contents

Words appearing in the text in bold, **like this**, are explained in the Glossary.

What is pollution?

Pollution happens when we add things that are harmful to the world around us. Some pollution is easy to see. Rubbish dropped as litter and smoke from a factory are pollution. Some pollution is harder to find. Clear, clean-looking water can be polluted with things you cannot see or taste.

Young people breathe more air, eat more food, and drink more water for their size than adults do. Many young people have decided to take action by helping to clean up pollution.

Everything in its place

Sometimes things that are good in one place are pollution in another. For example, soil in a forest provides a place for plants to grow, but when soil is washed into the ocean, it can pollute the water.

Some pollution comes from natural things that have become harmful. When a volcano erupts and sends ash around the world, the ash pollutes the air and land. However, people have made most of the pollution in our world. Today we know how to make less pollution. We also know how to clean a lot of it up.

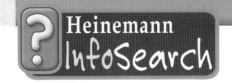

You can Save the Planet

Clean Planet: Stopping Litter and Pollution

Tristan Boyer Binns

www.heinemann.co.uk/library
Visit our website to find out more information about Heinemann Library books.

To order:
☎ Phone 44 (0) 1865 888066
🖨 Send a fax to 44 (0) 1865 314091
💻 Visit the Heinemann Bookshop at www.heinemann.co.uk/library to browse our catalogue and order online.

First published in Great Britain by Heinemann Library, Halley Court, Jordan Hill, Oxford OX2 8EJ, part of Harcourt Education. Heinemann is a registered trademark of Harcourt Education Ltd.

© Harcourt Education Ltd 2005
First published in paperback in 2006
The moral right of the proprietor has been asserted.

Editorial: Nancy Dickmann and Dave Harris
Design: Richard Parker and Q2A Solutions
Illustrations: Q2A and Jeff Edwards
Picture Research: Maria Joannou and Virginia Stroud-Lewis
Production: Camilla Smith

Originated by Dot Gradations Limited
Printed in China by WKT Company Limited

ISBN-10:   0 43104171 7 (hardback)
ISBN-13: 978 0 43104171 1 (hardback)
09 08 07 06
10 9 8 7 6 5 4 3 2

ISBN-10:   0 431 04177 6 (paperback)
ISBN-13: 978 0 431 04177 3 (paperback)
10 09 08 07 06
10 9 8 7 6 5 4 3 2 1

British Library Cataloguing in Publication Data
Binns, Tristan Boyer
Clean Planet: Stopping Litter and Pollution. – (You Can Save the Planet)
363.7'37
A full catalogue record for this book is available from the British Library.

Acknowledgements
The publishers would like to thank the following for permission to reproduce photographs: Alamy p. **8**; Alamy/Straw Hat p. **16**; Art Directors & Trip p. **25**; Corbis p. **11**; Corbis/Reuters pp. **23**, **24**, **27**; Corbis/Ed Young p. **12**; Corbis/John Brecher p. **10**; Corbis/John Hillery/Reuters p. **19**; Corbis/ML Sinibaldi/ p. **17**; Maria Joannou p. **18**; Michelin Photos/DPPI p. **26**; Mike Sheil p. **15**; NHPA/Stephen Dalton p. **27**; Panos Pictures/ Andy Johnstone p. **9**; Science Photo Library/David R. Frazier p. **5**; Science Photo Library/Mauro Fermariello pp. **13**, **21**; Science Photo Library/ Robert Brook p. **14**; Science Photo Library/Simon Fraser p. **6**; Topham Picturepoint p. **4**; Tudor Photography p. **20**; Vanessa Whelan p. **22**.

Cover photograph of children collecting litter, reproduced with permission of Topham Picturepoint/ Imageworks.

The publishers would like to thank Nick Lapthorn of the Field Studies Council for his assistance in the preparation of this book.

Every effort has been made to contact copyright holders of any material reproduced in this book. Any omissions will be rectified in subsequent printings if notice is given to the publishers.

The paper used to print this book comes from sustainable resources.

Disclaimer

What pollutes air and water?

Everyone needs air to breathe and water to drink, but sometimes air and water are polluted by chemicals. Some of the polluting chemicals we breathe and drink can make us ill. They can also harm other animals and plants.

In the air

Polluted air can make people, animals, and plants ill. It can change **ecosystems** so the living world does not work the way it should. Air pollution comes from things such as:

- power plants that burn **fuels** to make electricity
- the chemicals in things like petrol, cleaning fluids, and paint
- factory smoke
- cars, buses, lorries and aeroplanes that run on petrol or diesel
- wood-burning heaters and fireplaces
- rubbish being burned
- forest fires
- spray cans.

Pollution can make the air seem hazy. This is pollution over Los Angeles in the USA.

Particles and gases

Most air pollution is either tiny **particles** or chemical gases. The particles are so small and light you cannot see them as they float in the air. They can be made up of different things. Dust, sand, and the exhaust from diesel engines are all particles. Breathing in lots of particles can seriously damage a person's lungs.

Pollution can drift back down to Earth from the air. It can end up thousands of kilometres from where it was made. When it falls on to soil, plants take it in through their roots as they grow. Animals that eat polluted plants are then polluted too. Then when we eat them, we also eat the pollution.

Acid rain

Some air pollution gets into clouds and turns rainwater into an **acid**. **Acid rain** can kill plants and animals that other animals rely on for food. It can peel the paint on cars. It can wear down stone and brick buildings. Acid rain can fall very far from the source of its pollution. Some of the problems caused by acid rain are quick to appear. Others take a long time to see.

When acid rain falls on forests, it can change the soil so trees die.

Burning fuels

When **fossil fuels** are burned to make energy, they give off a gas called **carbon dioxide**. Carbon dioxide is not harmful to us – in fact, plants need it to make food for themselves. But we have made too much carbon dioxide which can change the Earth's **climate**.

Carbon dioxide has collected with other chemicals in a layer high up in the sky. This layer acts like the glass in a window. It lets the Sun's heat in but does not let it out again. This is called the greenhouse effect. The greenhouse effect makes the Earth warm up.

Science Behind It: The ozone layer

The **ozone layer** is high above the Earth. It protects us all from the Sun's rays, which can burn our skin and give us skin cancer. Some gas pollution that rises into the air reacts with strong sunlight. It eats away at the ozone layer. As the ozone layer thins, more of the Sun's rays get through to us. This is why it is important to protect yourself from the Sun with sunscreen, hats, and clothes.

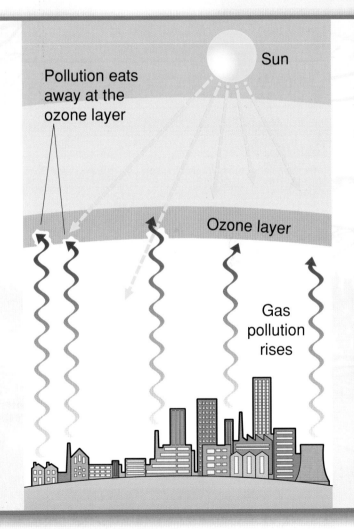

Sun

Pollution eats away at the ozone layer

Ozone layer

Gas pollution rises

Taking Action: Stopping pollution at home

Using less energy means fewer fossil fuels are burned. This means that less carbon dioxide and other polluting chemicals go into the air. You can save energy at school and home. Here is a list of some simple changes you can make, and how much carbon they will save. Carbon dioxide is measured in kilograms, even though it would be hard for you to weigh it on your scales at home!

Action	Carbon dioxide savings per year
Dry clothes on a line instead of in a dryer	353 kg (779 lb)
Turn off lights as you leave a room	171 kg (376 lb)
Turn heat down by about 1°C (2 °F)	160 kg (353 lb)
Run dishwasher only when it is full	91 kg (200 lb)
Turn off computers and TVs completely	62 kg (137 lb)
Plant a tree	6 kg (13 lb) per tree

Drying clothes on a line makes less pollution than using a tumble dryer – and it saves money too!

Water pollution

Factories use chemicals to make things. Some chemicals are left over as waste. They are usually treated to make them less dangerous. Then they are sent by pipes straight into oceans, rivers, and lakes.

We also put chemicals into the water when we use soaps and other cleaning products around the house. Even shampoo and laundry detergent change the water they run into. This makes it harder for plants and animals to live in the water.

Some pollution goes into the water from our streets and gardens. When it rains, oil on the streets and chemicals used on the land, such as **fertilizers** and **pesticides**, are washed away. They may run straight into a river or may go into the **storm drains** and **sewer system**. They will eventually drain into our water supply.

This stream is being polluted by waste chemicals from factories and the surrounding land.

Deep in the ground

Some chemicals get washed deeper into the earth. They sit in or near **groundwater**. When the groundwater is pumped out to be used for drinking water, the pollution comes out with it.

Pollution makes our water too dirty for us to drink or swim in. It can carry diseases to other people and animals. It can stop plants from growing. Animals that feed on those plants then have no food. Whole groups of plants and animals can die.

At home, make sure that any waste oil is taken away carefully. If it is poured into the drain, it will pollute the water near you.

Taking Action: Greener grass

Try talking with your parents and school about letting your grass grow longer. If it is longer, it will be stronger. Fewer weeds will grow in it. It still will look good without weed killer and fertilizer. It will need to be watered less in the summer. This means less water is wasted and fewer chemicals wash away.

What other kinds of pollution are there?

Some kinds of pollution can be easy to see, such as litter. Others are not so obvious. You may not have thought about sounds making pollution, but noise can also be a big problem.

The people living near this airport have to hear constant loud noise pollution.

Noise pollution

Most of us hear noise around us all the time. Sometimes it starts to make people and animals ill. Then it is called noise pollution. People can make it by playing loud music or shouting. Often noise pollution comes from cars on busy roads. Aeroplanes taking off and landing make a lot of noise pollution.

People have very sensitive ears. Noise pollution can damage hearing. People also become unhappy and can feel stress when they hear too much noise pollution. Children in schools near airports can have a hard time concentrating because of noise pollution.

Litter

Litter is any rubbish out of its proper place, even dog droppings. People do not like to see litter around where they live and work. It does not make people feel good about where they live. They may not want to go outside.

Litter can harm animals as well as looking bad. There are laws against dropping litter in many places.

When food and packaging is left on the streets and fields, animals and insects come to eat. Some spread diseases. Some get stuck in things such as bottles after they crawl in to get at the leftover drink. Broken glass can cut the animals if they step on it. Plastic bags get into fields and can hurt cows, sheep, and horses if they eat them. Old fishing lines can drown or strangle birds and fish.

Science Behind It: Roundworms

Some dog droppings have roundworms in them. Roundworms are parasites that live inside animals. However, roundworms can make you ill. They can get into you after you touch the droppings. That is why it is important to pick up after a dog wearing gloves or using a plastic bag. Always wash your hands after handling animals, to make sure nothing passes along to you.

How is pollution being cleaned up?

Some kinds of pollution, such as noise, can be stopped. Other kinds, such as chemicals and **particles**, never go away. Once we have made them, we can try to change them into safer kinds of chemicals. We can find ways to throw them away safely.

Legal fixes

Scientists are always working to learn more about chemicals and pollution. Sometimes they find new ways to clean up. The government then makes new laws to tell people and businesses what kinds of cleaning up they have to do. In power plants and factories, filters trap harmful chemicals. They are cleaned out of the **emissions** before they are let out into the air. The government sets the amounts of chemicals that are allowed to escape the filters and go into the air.

This scientist is collecting a water sample so he can study the amount of pollution in it.

Science Behind It: Cleaning with algae

Scientists have bred algae that eat **carbon dioxide** as their food. They use the algae to eat some of the carbon dioxide gas from power plants. The gas is bubbled through water where the algae live. When the algae cannot eat any more, they can be used as non-polluting **fertilizer**.

Waste and pollution

When we make waste, we need somewhere to put it. Most of it goes into a big pit called a landfill. Landfill sites give off methane gas that adds to **climate change**. Even food scraps in a landfill turn into **toxic** liquid. The pollution then seeps down into the **groundwater**. A good way to clean up a landfill is not to add to it in the first place. People can cut their household waste a great deal by **recycling** and **composting**.

Incinerators can be used to burn some of the landfill waste so it takes up less space. Some people think this helps clean it up. But incinerators make toxic smoke and still create ash to put back into the landfill.

This is an incinerator at a landfill site. It is better to create less waste than to put it in landfill sites or burn it!

Natural cleaning

Trees and plants help clean the air. They take carbon dioxide out of the air, and also suck up other polluting gases and particles. People in towns can plant trees outside. Houseplants help clean the air inside. The best houseplants are ivies, palms, peace lilies, and chrysanthemums.

Cleaning up water

Cleaning up water can be hard. Polluted rivers and streams are treated in a few ways. First the source of the pollution has to be stopped. Trees and water plants that belong in the river are planted. Places are made for animals and fish to live.

Particles in water are called sediment. Some sediment is polluted. When it sinks to the bottom of the water, it can be sucked up and cleaned. The source of pollution has to be stopped so the water is not polluted again.

Spilled oil floating on top of water can be trapped and sucked into containers to be taken away. Rubbish and litter in water has to be picked up. In the middle of a large body of water, ships are used to collect it.

These workers are trying to clean up oil pollution in Russia.

Taking Action: Litter pick

Streets, rivers, and beaches polluted with litter can be cleaned up. You can look around where you live and see where litter is a problem. Working with adults, organize a 'litter pick'. Make sure you wear gloves and are safe while you are picking up litter! You can recycle the litter or throw it away properly.

Case Study: Eco School in Wales

In South Wales, the school Ysgol Y Gwendraeth is working on stopping litter and pollution. Their eco-club runs many activities. One member even went to speak with Prime Minister Tony Blair. They talked about why schools are not run in ways that are more Earth-friendly.

Reduce-Reuse-Recycle fashion show

Students and teachers modelled reused clothing from local charity shops. The show also featured hats and other clothes made by students using **recycled** plastic, bin bags, and carrier bags. Pupils had to pay to see the show with a piece of plastic. These were collected for recycling. It was such a success that more fashion shows are planned.

If you have a litter clean-up at school, make sure you wear gloves.

The eco-club also ran litter clean-ups. Students wrote their names on rubbish as they dropped it in the bins. Four winners were drawn from the bins. Each won £5. Two classes of eleven-year-old boys had a big litter clean-up in the school grounds. After one and a half hours, 22 boys had collected 36 kilograms of litter!

CASE STUDY

How can we stop pollution in the first place?

It is probably easier to stop pollution than it is to try and clean it up. People and governments around the world are working on pollution prevention. By learning about pollution and telling people what we know we are helping too. **Campaigning** to change the ways things are done can make a big difference.

Energy from wind power is renewable and easy to use.

Better power

One thing we are all part of is changing the way our energy is made. Most countries have agreed to use more **renewable** sources for their power. Renewable sources cause far less pollution than **fossil fuels**, and some may not pollute at all. Wind and solar power are good examples. You can ask your electricity company what they are doing to help. You can change to a company that is using more renewable **fuels**.

Better choices

We can stop pollution by choosing less polluting products. For example, you can choose to use **biodegradable** cleaning products with no polluting chemicals in them. This means you create less pollution when you clean your house or clothes.

Big companies can help out by changing the way they make things. If they reduce the amount of materials used in packaging, there will be less to make. Making less means less pollution. There will also be less to throw away. For example, plastic drinks bottles are now made with less plastic than they were 25 years ago. They now weigh 17 grams less, which is about the weight of a bite of chocolate bar. This means that every year over 100 million kilograms of plastic is saved.

Businesses can help stop waste in their offices too, by making sure that paper gets recycled.

Better engines

Roads and engines are loud. One way to reduce the noise pollution from roads is to make barriers that absorb the sound. Engines are always being improved. Newer ones not only use less fuel, but also make less noise. Aircraft engines are up to 70 per cent quieter than they used to be.

Cars make a lot of pollution. Governments are making laws that say fuels and engines must be cleaner. They are also helping people to switch their cars to cleaner fuels. **Grant** money helps pay for filters for bus engines. Grants can help people pay for new cleaner cars as well.

Science Behind It: Cleaner cars

Special machines called catalytic converters take pollution out of engine fumes. They are filters coated with metals. The engine's exhaust goes into the catalytic converter. The metals change some of the harmful chemicals into ones that are safe. The catalytic converter also burns any unused fuel so that the most harmful parts of it are used up. Then it lets the exhaust out into the air.

Some new **hybrid** cars like this one have petrol engines and powerful batteries too. They give off no pollution while they run on their batteries.

Thinking and acting

You can stop pollution by thinking carefully about what you buy.

- Look at how things are packaged – is there more than is needed? Extra packaging gives off pollution as it is made and adds to landfill when you throw it away.
- Read the labels – do you know what all the chemicals listed do? Will they pollute the Earth or your body?
- Look at where things were made – have they travelled a long way? Transporting things makes pollution from exhaust fumes.
- Do you even need a new thing, or do you have something that can be repaired instead? Making new things causes pollution, and throwing something out adds to landfill.

Special bins called dog toilets can help stop dog droppings from becoming a problem.

No more litter!

Sometimes people do not think about littering. They just do it. Posters can remind them to use a rubbish bin instead. One campaign gives people a famous face to stick their used chewing gum onto! Towns need to give us enough rubbish bins in the right places too.

Taking Action: Stopping pollution with food

Look at the food in your home and see where it came from. Read the labels on fresh and stored foods. Think about the pollution that was made to bring you that food. How can you change what you buy and reduce pollution?

- Growing your own **organic** food means fewer **emissions** in transport, less waste in packaging, and fewer **fertilizers** and **pesticides**.
- If you cannot do that, ask your parents and school to buy locally grown food. It travels less distance so pollutes less in transport.
- If enough of your friends and neighbours want local food, you can create demand. A box-delivery scheme, with food direct from farmers, is one answer. Another is local farmers' markets where the people who grow the food also sell it.

This is a shopping basket full of organic food. The food has been made without using any polluting chemicals.

Case Study: Waste Wise Schools in Australia

The Australian Capital Territory (ACT) is the area around the capital city of Canberra. The government has set a goal of zero waste by 2010. This will cut pollution a lot, and save everyone money. Part of this is the Waste Wise Schools programme. Almost half of the 200 schools in the ACT have joined in. They are all **recycling** everything they can. Here are two schools with some interesting ideas.

Farrer Primary School

Farrer has an Environmental Centre with garden beds, **compost** heaps, special worm farms, chickens, and other animals. All the food scraps in the school are fed to the animals. Students in each classroom put scraps into separate containers for worms and chickens. The compost heaps make good natural **fertilizer** for the gardens. Vegetables grown in the gardens are sold back to the students for them to eat.

Holy Trinity Primary School

Here students have No Waste Lunch Days. Only reusable packaging is used, so there are no wrappers to throw away. No waste means no litter as well. They also made and sold their own cloth carrier bags that say 'Waste Busters'. People can use these instead of plastic carrier bags that cause pollution when they are made, and add to landfill when thrown away.

How can we stop pollution from cars?

Much of the world's pollution comes from vehicles with engines. When an engine burns petrol or diesel it puts polluting **emissions** into the air. With more and more cars being sold, the amount of pollution will go up if we do not work to stop it.

What to do?

The question is how to keep moving people from one place to another while reducing pollution. There are many answers.

- Look at other ways to get where you need to go. Walking and cycling whenever you can saves pollution, and also keeps you fit. Governments can help by making more safe routes to follow.
- **Public transport** such as buses and trains use less fuel per person using them. Governments can help by making sure there are bus and train routes with good services.
- If you have to go by car, try to share rides. Your local council may have a scheme to match people up for regular journeys. Families living near each other can share lifts to school and work.

These cars are taking part in a solar car race. They burn no fuel, which means they make no polluting emissions.

Reducing pollution from cars

People can think about how they use their cars to reduce the amount of pollution they make.

- A car's engine is at its best and least polluting when it is serviced on time.
- Speed limits are not just about safety. A car going above 70 miles per hour creates four times the pollution it did at speeds below 70 miles per hour!
- A change to the fuel can help. City petrol and city diesel have the polluting chemical sulphur taken out. They give off less pollution as they are burned.
- Some engines can be run on **alternative fuels**. **Biofuels**, natural gas and **propane** can give off less pollution. Some engines can be changed to run on these fuels.
- A different kind of engine may be the answer. Electric engines are run by solar panels, batteries, or fuel cells. Making electricity can give off pollution. But once the battery or fuel cell is charged, an electric car does not give off any pollution where it drives. This can help make the air cleaner in cities.

This is an alternative fuel station in San Diego, USA. It has a classroom so people can learn about alternative fuels!

Getting to school

School is often close to home. Cars give off the most pollution during the first three kilometres (two miles) that they drive. So the short drive to school makes a lot of pollution. In Denmark, people got so worried about pollution that they made special safe cycle routes to school. Now over half of all Danish children cycle to school. All over the world, there are 'walking buses' where children join a snake of others all on their way to school. Parents take turns walking with the bus.

In the USA, school buses drive 5 billion miles each year. People worry about the buses' emissions. Some school districts are changing their buses to alternative fuels.

Taking Action: Clean transport

Make a list of all the journeys you make each week. Pick one day to change then decide how to do it. Can you share rides, start a walking bus, or go by bike? Remember that your changes have to be safe and practical too!

These children are walking safely to school in a walking bus.

Case Study: Green school buses

The school buses in the Northside School District in Texas in the USA together drive about 12 million kilometres (8 million miles) a year. Most run on **propane** instead of petrol. This saves over US$1000 (£565) a year per bus. The buses last longer as well. They use less motor oil and give off 65 per cent fewer **emissions** than buses that run on petrol.

This school bus is powered by electricity. It is being driven at a race track to see how fast it can go!

free and better

In 1992 in Lancaster, California, the school buses all ran on diesel **fuel**. They were fined US$3000 (£1700) each day because the emissions were so polluted. Now about a third of the buses run on **alternative** fuels. The new buses were all paid for by **grants** from California's energy and air quality agencies. The most popular bus is the electric one. It is so quiet that people ask why it is not making any noise!

What is going on around you?

In every community there are issues about pollution and litter. By being aware of what is happening in your local area, you can help make the future cleaner for everyone.

Clearwater

The Hudson River in New York is an important waterway. It has suffered badly from pollution. The Clearwater Project works with local people and the government. The goal is to get the river clean enough for people, animals, and fish. Scientists and volunteers work together on research and **campaigns**. They have festivals too. People can come aboard the wooden ship *Clearwater* to learn more and help with research.

Taking Action

What is happening in your area? How can you help change it for the better? One good place to start is with your local Friends of the Earth group. They run local campaigns on airports, transport, and many other topics. You could find out more in your local newspaper. You can write letters to the editor to get your voice heard.

This member of Friends of the Earth is campaigning to reduce pollution and improve the quality of the air in Hong Kong.

fact file

- About 560 million cars are driving on the world's roads. Older cars use more **fuel** and create more pollution than new ones.
- About one-fifth of all the **carbon dioxide** in the UK and one-sixth in Australia comes from transport.
- In Denmark, 60% of children cycle to school. In the UK, fewer than 3% do.
- **Recycling** one aluminium can saves enough energy to run a TV for three hours.
- We produce 20 times more plastic today than we did 50 years ago.
- About half of all household rubbish is packaging.
- About half of our rubbish can be reused or recycled, instead of being thrown away.
- In Canberra, Australia, the town has Second Hand Sundays. People put out the stuff they do not want any more. Anyone can come and take it for free!
- Litter surveys show that about half of all the litter on beaches is plastic.
- Over 20,000 water bodies across the USA are polluted. Most Americans live within 16 kilometres (10 miles) of one of these polluted water bodies.
- Our bodies now contain over 300 chemicals that they did not only 60 years ago.

find out more

Books to read

Earth's Precious Resources: Air, Ian Graham (Heinemann Library, 2004)

Green Files: Polluted Planet, Steve Parker (Heinemann Library, 2004)

Websites

There are many useful websites to help you learn more and make plans for taking action of your own.

Friends of the Earth — the website of this major international organization has lots of information about projects and campaigns:
www.foei.org

The Environment Agency — information about many issues. They have special kids' pages too:
www.environment-agency.gov.uk

Tidy Britain — a useful site full of information about stopping littering:
www.tidybritain.org.uk

Waste Watch — information about waste in general:
www.wastewatch.org.uk

The Reef Guardian Schools Program — information on cleaning up the Great Barrier Reef:
www.reefed.edu.au

Waste Wise Schools — information on some schools that are making a difference:
www.nowaste.act.gov.au/ed/schools.html

Glossary

acid sour, can dissolve metal

acid rain rainwater that has been turned into acid by picking up chemicals

alternative something different from what is usually used. An alternative fuel is something other than petrol or diesel.

biodegradable something that breaks down completely naturally without causing harm when thrown or washed away

biofuel fuel made from plants, such as sugar cane or used vegetable oil

campaign series of things done by a group of people to achieve a result

carbon dioxide gas made from carbon and oxygen that adds to climate change. It is also used by plants to make their food.

climate what the temperature, wind, humidity, rainfall, and other weather is like in an area

climate change as we add to the layer of gases that surround Earth, different climates around the world may get warmer or colder, wetter or dryer. No one is sure how much change will happen.

compost material that helps plants grow, which is made from the remains of rotting plants

ecosystem place and all the different living things that live there together make an ecosytem

efficient using a resource, such as energy or water, so that as little as possible is wasted

emissions chemicals and fumes that are given off when fuel is burned, for example from a car engine or a factory

fertilizer chemical that helps plants grow

fossil fuel fuel that is formed from the remains of plants and animals that died millions of years ago. Fossil fuels include coal, gas, and oil.

fuel thing that can be burned to create heat or power

grant money given to help buy or change something, such as changing the kind of fuel an engine uses to a less polluting one

groundwater water held below the surface of the Earth

hybrid made up of two things. For example, a hybrid car uses both petrol and battery power.

incinerator place where waste is burned

organic describes food raised or grown without using chemicals such as fertilizers and pesticides

ozone layer part of the atmosphere that goes all around the Earth. The ozone layer blocks many of the Sun's harmful rays.

particle very small piece of something

pesticide chemical that kills pests such as insects

propane kind of fossil fuel that is compressed into cans

public transport buses, trains, trams, and any kind of transport that can be used by many people at once

recycle collect things made from a material that can be broken down and remade into new things, such as newspapers, plastic or glass bottles

renewable something that does not run out when we use it, such as solar energy

sewer system network of pipes that all liquid waste travels through, usually to a water treatment plant

storm drain drain that collects the water that runs off pavements and roads when it rains

toxic poisonous

Index